My Garden

by Nicholas Spencer
illustrated by Mary Newell DePalma

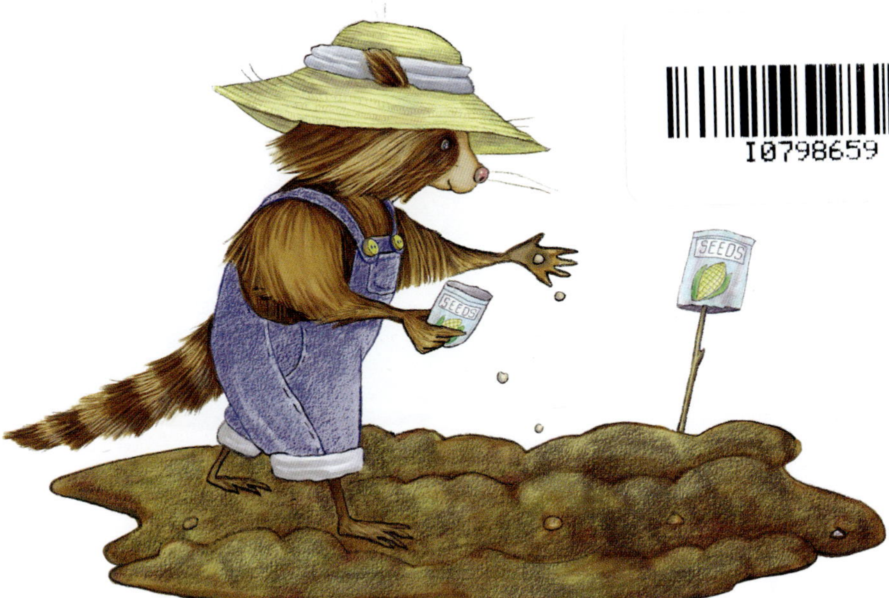

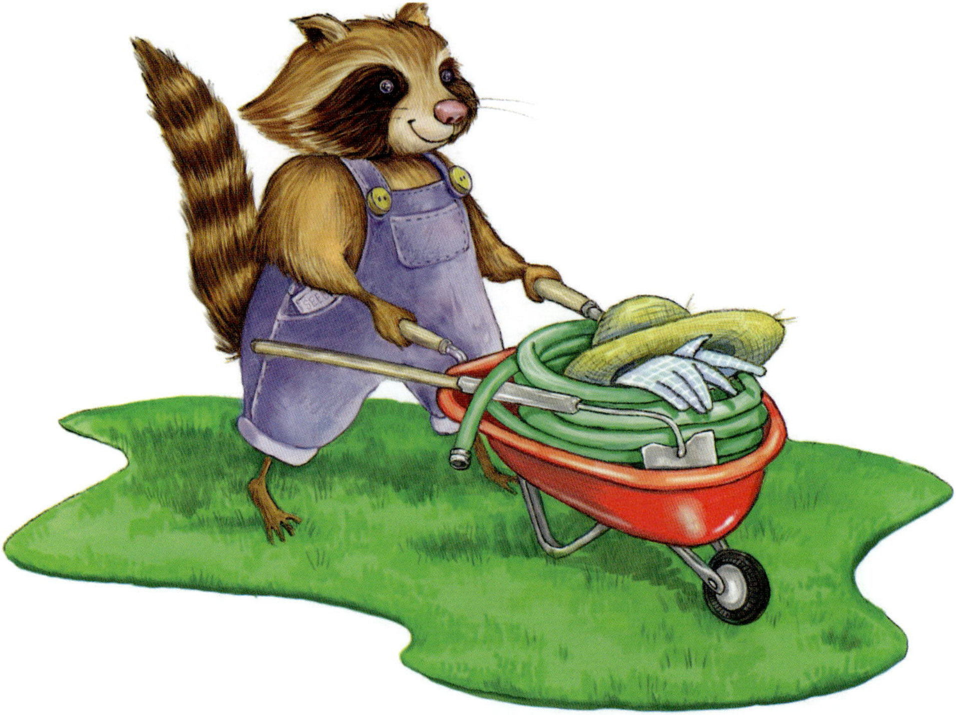

I like my 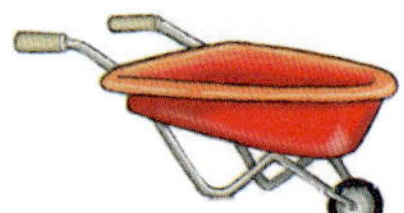 wheelbarrow .

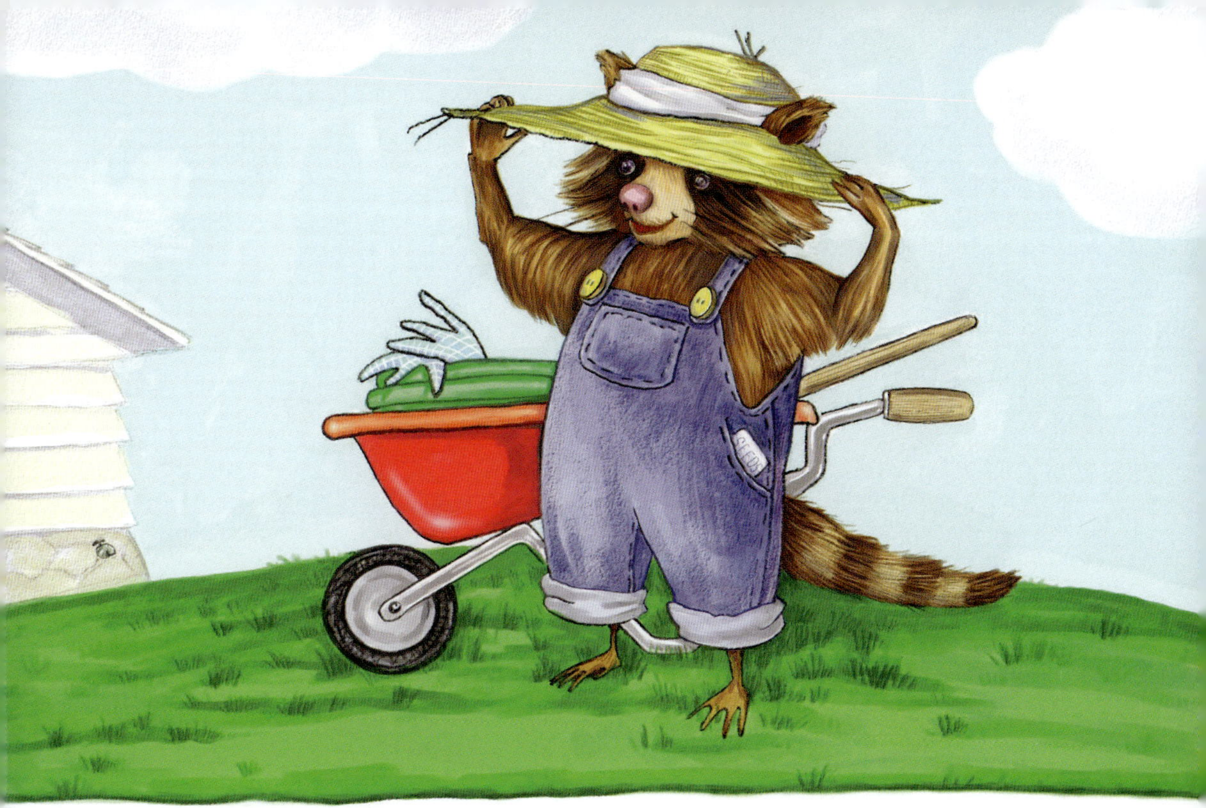

I like my 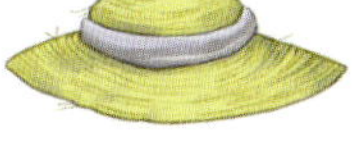 hat .

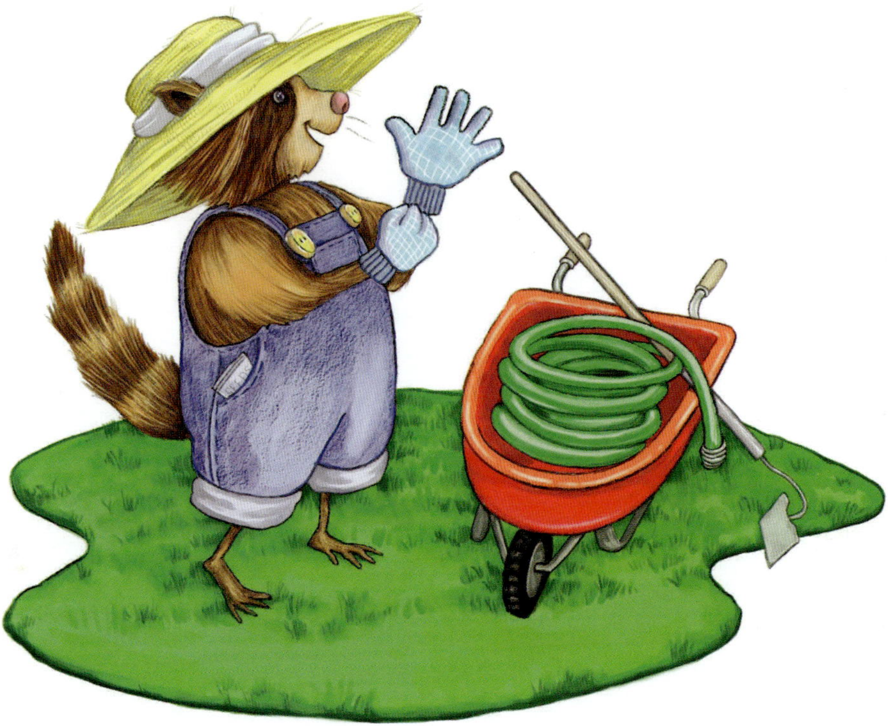

I like my 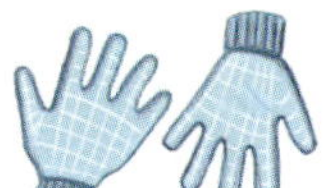 gloves .

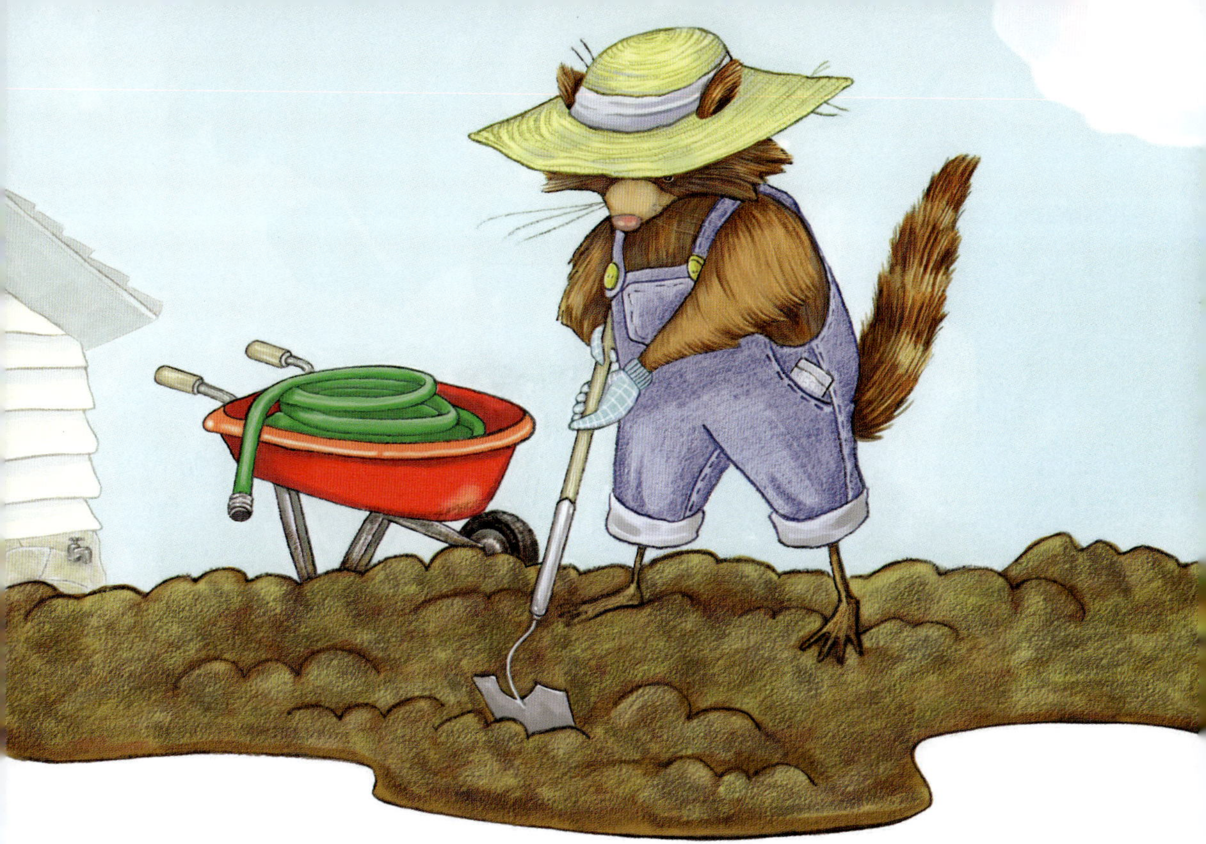

I like my 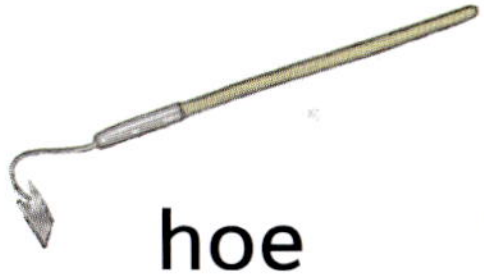 hoe.

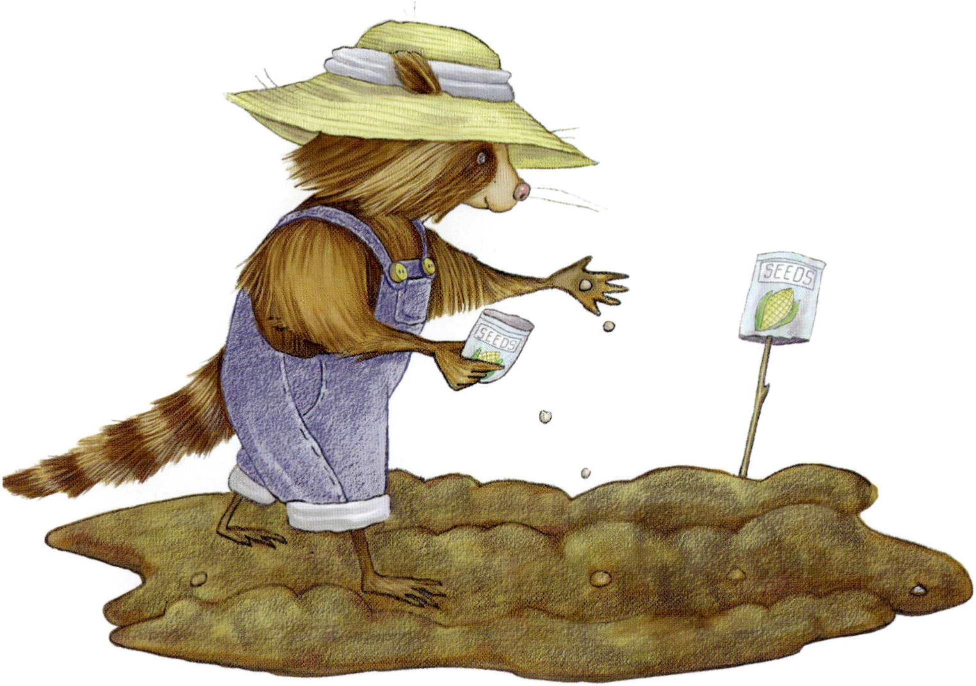

I like my 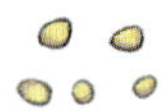 seeds .

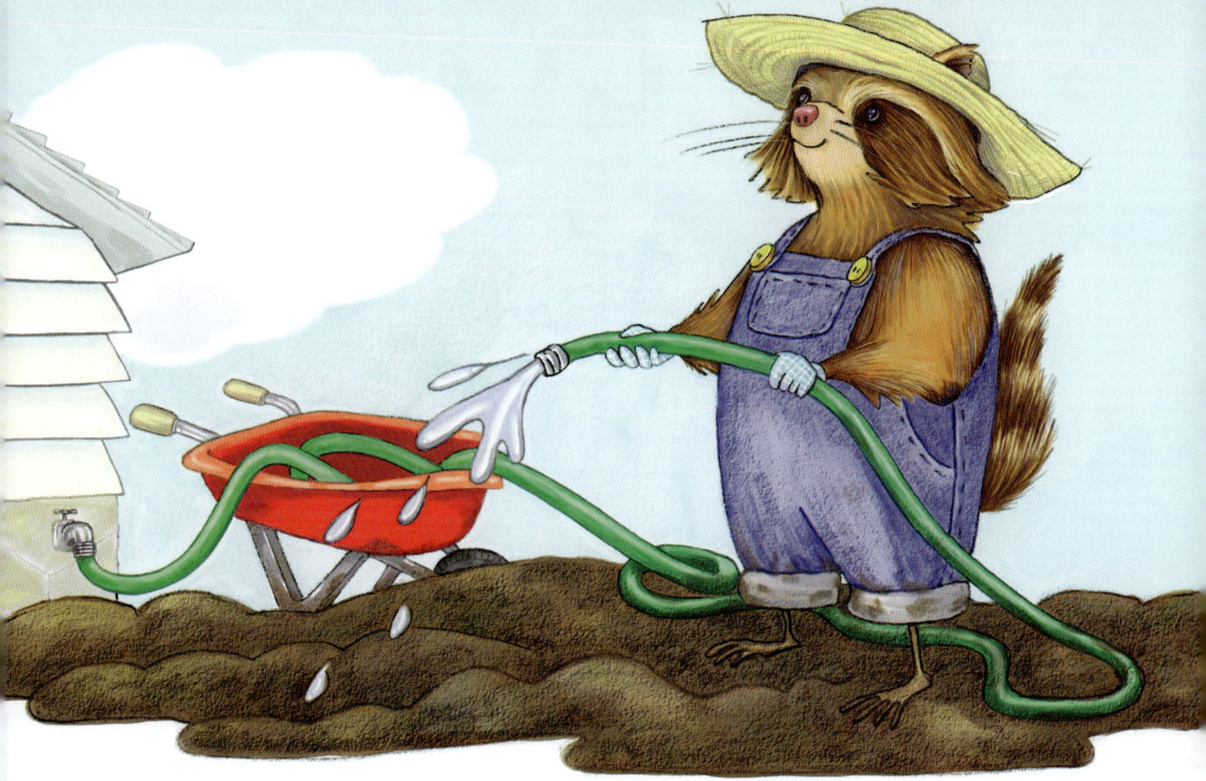

I like my 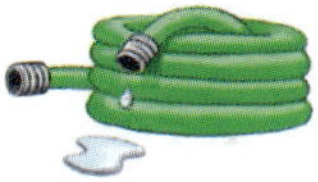 hose .

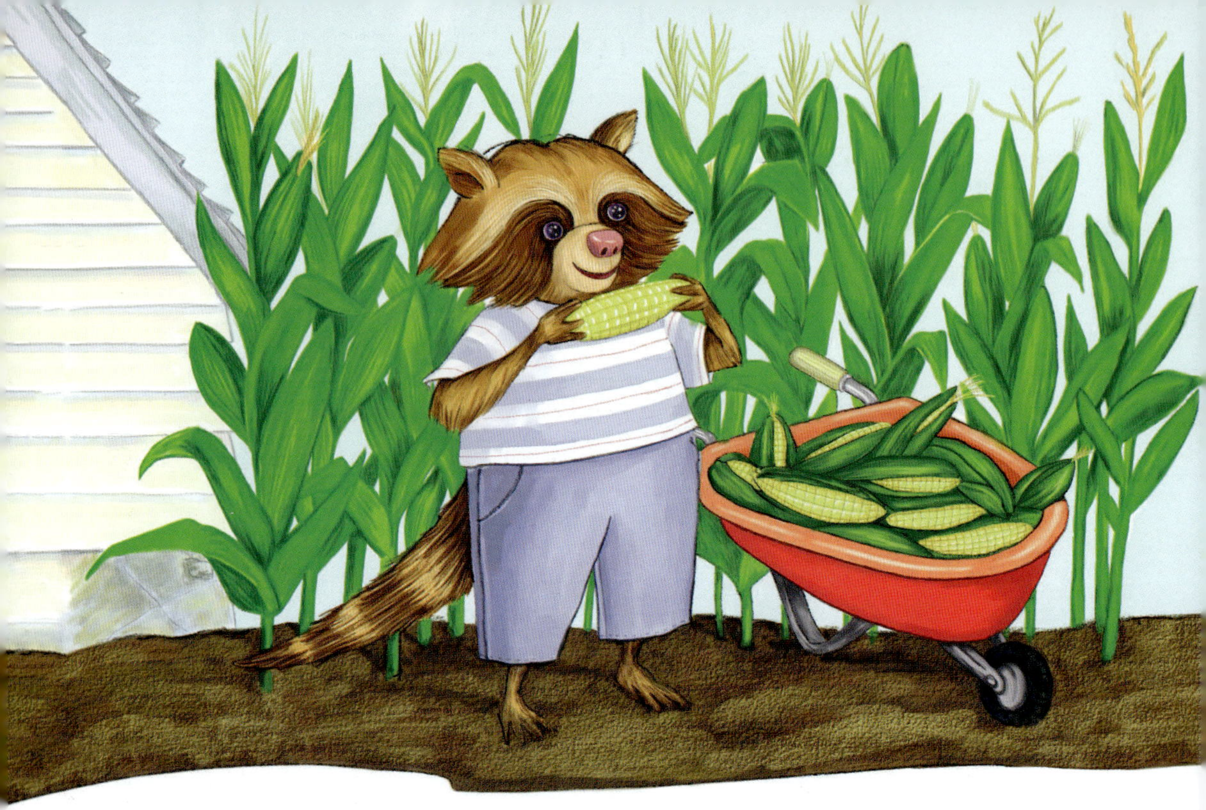

I like my fat 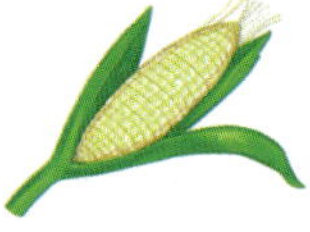 corn !